h: 1.8
Pts 0.5

Pebble™

Polar Animals

Seals

harp seal pup

by Emily Rose Townsend

Consulting Editor: Gail Saunders-Smith, Ph.D.
Consultant: Brock R. McMillan, Ph.D.
Associate Professor, Department of Biological Sciences
Minnesota State University, Mankato

Capstone
press
Mankato, Minnesota

Pebble Books are published by Capstone Press
151 Good Counsel Drive, P.O. Box 669, Mankato, Minnesota 56002
www.capstonepress.com

1 2 3 4 5 6 09 08 07 06 05 04

Library of Congress Cataloging-in-Publication Data
Townsend, Emily Rose.
　　Seals / by Emily Rose Townsend.
　　p. cm.—(Polar animals)
　　Includes bibliographical references and index.
　　Contents: Seals—What seals do—Body parts.
　　ISBN 0-7368-2359-X (hardcover)
　　1. Seals (Animals)—Juvenile literature. [1. Seals (Animals)] I. Title.
QL737.P6T73 2004
599.79—dc21
　　　　　　　　　　　　　　　　　　　　　　　　　　　　　　2003011426

Note to Parents and Teachers

The Polar Animals series supports national science standards related to life science. This book describes and illustrates seals. The photographs support early readers in understanding the text. The repetition of words and phrases helps early readers learn new words. This book also introduces early readers to subject-specific vocabulary words, which are defined in the Glossary. Early readers may need assistance to read some words and to use the Table of Contents, Glossary, Read More, Internet Sites, and Index/Word List sections of the book.

Table of Contents

4

Seals

Seals are marine
mammals. Seals
have whiskers.

northern fur seal

Seals live in seas
and oceans.

bearded seal

land where seals live

other areas where seals live

8

Many seals live
in the Antarctic
and Arctic Oceans.

What Seals Do

Seals can breathe
through holes in the ice.

harp seal and pup

Seals come to land
to lie in the sun
and to give birth.

harp seal pup

14

Seals eat fish, squid, and krill.

gray seal

Body Parts

Seals have fur
and blubber to
keep them warm.

harp seal pup

flipper →

18

Seals have flippers
that help them swim.

bearded seal

20

Seals have big eyes.
Seals can see at night
and deep in the ocean.

Weddell seal

Glossary

Antarctic—a cold area around the South Pole

Arctic—a cold area around the North Pole

blubber—fat under the skin of some marine animals; blubber keeps animals warm.

flipper—a flat limb with bones on a sea animal; flippers help seals swim.

krill—tiny animals that are similar to shrimp

mammal—a warm-blooded animal with a backbone and hair or fur

ocean—a large body of salt water

sea—an area of salt water that is part of an ocean; seas are partly enclosed by land.

squid—a sea animal with a long, soft body and 10 finger-like arms used to grasp food

whisker—a long, stiff hair near the mouth of some mammals; seals use their whiskers to feel.

Read More

Parker, Steve. *Seal.* Natural World. Chicago: Raintree, 2003.

Rotter, Charles. *Seals.* Naturebooks. Chanhassen, Minn.: Child's World, 2001.

Rustad, Martha E. H. *Seals.* Ocean Life. Mankato, Minn.: Pebble Books, 2001.

Internet Sites

FactHound offers a safe, fun way to find Internet sites related to this book. All of the sites on FactHound have been researched by our staff.

Here's how:

1. Visit *www.facthound.com*
2. Type in this special code **073682359X** for age-appropriate sites. Or enter a search word related to this book for a more general search.
3. Click on the **Fetch It** button.

FactHound will fetch the best sites for you!

Index/Word List

Word Count: 79
Early-Intervention Level: 12

Editorial Credits
Mari C. Schuh, editor; Patrick D. Dentinger, designer; Scott Thoms, photo researcher; Karen Risch, product planning editor

Photo Credits
Corbis, cover
Florian Graner/Seapics, 14
Laura N. Scott Imagery, 8
Minden Pictures/Flip Nicklin, 6, 18; Michio Hoshino, 10; Mitsuaki Iwago, 1; Norbert Wu, 20
Robin Brandt, 4
Tom Stack & Associates/Jeff Foott, 12, 16